The day of the science fair was finally here! And Cindy Cadoodle was ready. You see, she'd invented a great gadget and couldn't wait to show it off. It was called the Totally Terrific Turbo-Charged Mega-Deluxe Capitalization Machine.

"How does that contraption work?" Bonnie Brickle asked.

"Allow me to demonstrate," said Cindy. She wrote Bonnie's name on a piece of paper.

"That's wrong. You made it all lowercase!" exclaimed Bonnie.

Rule #1:
People's first, middle, and last names always begin with capital letters.

"Just watch," responded Cindy. With that, she fed the paper into her invention. The machine bleeped and blipped and gurgled. Then out popped her name with the proper capitalization.

"Wow!" screeched Bonnie. "Your invention really works!"

"Let me try! Let me try!" shouted Gary Grigsby.

"Make sure you write in all lowercase," said Cindy. Gary wrote down his favorite month, day of the week, and holiday.

Rule #2:
Days of the week, months, and holidays are always capitalized.

The machine beeped and blared and chortled. Then out popped the words with the proper capitalization. "That's awesome!" exclaimed Gary.

"My turn," said Olivia Orlando. Olivia was a world traveler. Her family always went on fantastic vacations. Olivia closed her eyes and thought about a place she dreamed of visiting. She wrote down the city, country, and even the continent.

Rule #3:
The names of cities, countries, and continents always begin with capital letters.

Cindy's invention jumped and gibbered and yodeled. Then out popped the words with the proper capitalization. "Ooh-la-la!" remarked Olivia enthusiastically.

Now it was Henry Hilbert's turn. Henry loved history. It was his favorite subject. He wrote down three fascinating historical events.

Rule #4:
Important historical events, such as the Boston Tea Party or Civil War, always begin with capital letters.

The machine sniffed and snorted and crackled. Then out popped the words with the proper capitalization. "Simply sensational," stated Henry.

"Don't forget me!" squealed Dina Duncan. Dina was always up on the latest trends. She wrote down her favorite book, movie, and rock band.

Rule #5:
The names of books, movies, and rock bands should be capitalized. The same goes for other kinds of entertainment such as plays, TV shows, magazines, and sports teams.

The invention rocked and rattled and clattered. Then out popped the words with the proper capitalization. "Utterly fabu!" declared Dina. "By the way, that's the newest way to say *great*."

Freddie Farber loved ice cream. He also loved cookies, popcorn, lollipops, potato chips, beef jerky, soda, and bubble gum. Freddie wrote the names of his three favorite snacks in the whole world.

Rule #6:
Brand names of various items, such as snacks and toys, should be capitalized.

The machine gulped and gobbled and burped. Then out popped the words with the proper capitalization. "Mouthwatering!" cried Freddie.

Now it was the science teacher's turn to examine the machine. Cindy was very nervous. Mr. Menlo circled her invention, pushing buttons and twisting dials. After a few minutes, he announced: "Brilliant! Remarkable! Ingenious!" Then, quick as a wink, he jotted something on a piece of paper and fed it into the machine.

The invention clanged and clapped and whistled. Then out popped the paper. On it, Mr. Menlo had written a single big, bold letter. It was Cindy's grade for the science fair project—an A+. Talk about a capital day!

Remember to always capitalize...

1. the first letter of first, middle, and last names

2. days of the week, months, and holidays

3. places, cities, countries, and continents

4. important historical events

5. books, movies, plays, TV shows, magazines, bands, and sport's teams

6. brand names, including snacks and toys

Got it? Great. Now, brainstorm a list of words that fit in each category. Don't forget to capitalize them!